Levers

written by Caroline Rush
and
illustrated by Mike Gordon

Wayland

Simple Technology

Wheels and Cogs
Slopes
Levers
Pulleys

Series Editor: Catherine Baxter
Advice given by Phil Cornish
First published in 1996 by
Wayland (Publishers) Ltd
61 Western Road, Hove,
East Sussex, BN3 1JD, England

British Library Cataloguing in Publication Data
Rush Caroline
Levers. - (Simple Technology)
1. Levers - Juvenile literature
I. Title
621.811

ISBN 0750218355

Typeset by MacGuru
Printed and bound in Italy by G Canale and C.S.p.A., Turin, Italy

Contents

We use machines
everyday to help us to
do all sorts of things.
Some machines are big
and complicated.

Some are very simple.

A lever is probably
one of the simplest
machines there is.

A lever can make moving something easier. This is because it can turn a small force into a bigger force. A force is the energy that makes something move. Pushing and pulling are both forces.

FORCE

Take a ball of plasticine in your hands. Push and pull it into different shapes.

The force, or pushing and pulling, of your fingers makes the plasticine move.

FORCE

Levers were probably first used by Stone Age people. They may have moved heavy rocks by using branches as levers.

Try this for yourself. Find a strong stick and put one end under a heavy cardboard box. Next, push a smaller object under the stick (for the stick to rest on).

Press down on the top end of the stick.
Can you see how the bottom end
is forced up, making the box move?

A lever has three parts.

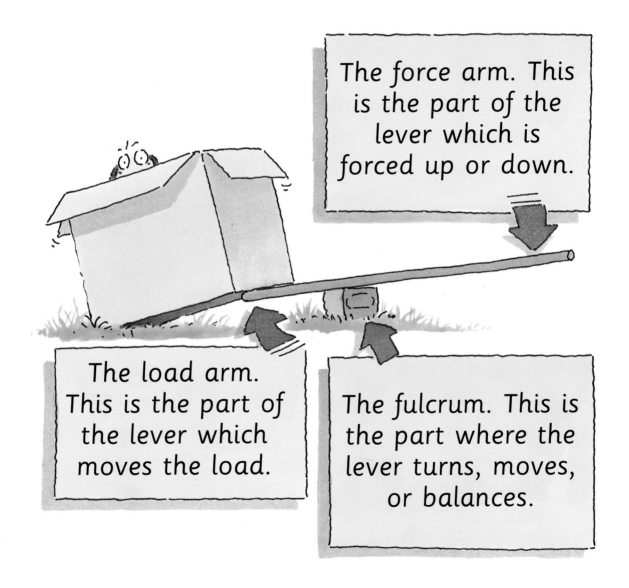

The force arm. This is the part of the lever which is forced up or down.

The load arm. This is the part of the lever which moves the load.

The fulcrum. This is the part where the lever turns, moves, or balances.

You probably use lots of levers.

At your desk....

In the garden...

around the house...

in the garage.

A lever can be very useful for a burglar!

15

When you go to the park you may even sit
on a lever!

A seesaw is a lever. When you sit on one
end, your weight acts as a force. It pushes
your end down and the other end up. Two
children of about the same weight can move
the ends of a seesaw up and down!

Make a seesaw.
Rest a long plank of wood on a brick.
(Make sure the brick is in the middle.)
The place where the brick rests
on the plank is the fulcrum.

What happens if two children sit on one end of the seesaw lever?

Move the brick towards the end of the seesaw with the heavier weight. What happens now?

A light weight can lift a heavy weight if the heavy weight is near to the fulcrum.

Levers come in all sorts of
useful shapes and sizes.

A wheelbarrow is a lever. The wheel acts as the fulcrum. When you pull up the handles, this small force can lift a heavy load.

A nutcracker is also a lever. The fulcrum is where the two arms join at one end. When you push the two arms together, this small force turns into a greater force nearer to the fulcrum. This crushes the nut.

A pair of tongs is a slightly different lever. You squeeze the tongs, or apply a force in the middle. This allows the tongs to hold an object in place.

Some parts of your body are levers. Your arms are levers which can lift heavy weights.

Your muscles apply a force which moves the bones in your arms up and down. Your elbow joint acts as a fulcrum.

Some levers don't lift weights - they just move things up and down.

Make a snappy crocodile puppet with a lever jaw.

You will need:
Stiff card
2 brass split pins
1 piece of wooden dowling
Sticky tape

1. Cut out a crocodile shape. Separate the jaw piece, and cut a separate strip of card.

a.

b.

c.

2. Join the jaw piece and card strip with a split pin.

3. Join the jaw piece to the body with the other split pin.

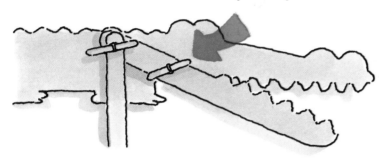

4. Attach the wooden dowling with sticky tape, to use as a handle.

5. Pull the card strip to make the crocodile's jaws snap!

Glossary

Energy   The power to do work.

Force   A push or pull on an object.

Force arm   The part of the lever to which the force is applied.

Fulcrum   The point on which a lever balances or turns.

Load   The weight of the object that is to be moved by the lever.

Load arm   The part of a lever which moves the load.

Machine   A device to make work easier.

Books to read

Machines at Work by Alan Ward (Watts, 1993)
Starting Technology/Machines by John Williams (Wayland, 1991)
How Things Work by Brian Knapp (Atlantic Europe Publishing, 1991)
The Way It Works by Philip Sauvain (Heinemann, 1991)
Experiment With Movement by Brian Murphy (Watts, 1991)
Simple Science/Push and Pull by Mike and Maria Gordon (Wayland, 1995)

Adult Reference
The Way Things Work by David Macaulay (Dorling Kindersley, 1988)

Notes for adults

Simple Technology is a series of elementary books designed to introduce children to the everyday machines which make all of our lives easier, and the basic principles behind them.

For millions of years people have been inventing and using machines to make work easier. These machines have been constantly modified and redesigned over the years to make them more sophisticated and more successful at their task. This is really what technology is all about. It is the process of applying knowledge to make work easier.

In these books, children are encouraged to explore the early inspirations for machines and the process of modification which has brought them forward to their current state, and in so doing, come to an understanding of the design process.

The simple text and humorous illustrations give a clear explanation of how these machines actually work and experiments and activities give suggestions for further practical exploration.

Suggestions for further activities

* Make a collection of levers and encourage children to test them out.
* Explore the principle of force, including different ways of creating a force.
* To further examine how a lever can multiply a force, encourage children to design an experiment which tests the effect of changing the distance between fulcrum, load and effort. Record and analyse results.
* Divide levers into first, second and third class, and compare their properties.

Index